Includes Five SAT Words to Know
MEETS STATE AND NATIONAL STANDARDS
Japan
An Island Country of Endless Intrigue!
IT'S YOUR WORLD
LIVE
WORK
PLAY
LEARN
Where Do You Want to Go?
Hey! It's the Kinkakuji Temple! Do you want to go?
By Carole Marsh

Live • Work • Play • Learn

GALLOPADE INTERNATIONAL

Gallopade International is introducing SAT words that kids need to know in our books. The SAT words in this book have a gray box around them. Students can look up the definitions and increase their vocabulary. Happy Learning!

Gallopade is proud to be a member and supporter of these educational organizations and associations:

Association for the Study of African American Life and History
National Alliance of Black School Educators
American Booksellers Association
American Library Association
International Reading Association
National Association for Gifted Children
The National School Supply and Equipment Association
The National Council for the Social Studies
Museum Store Association
Association of Partners for Public Lands
Association of Booksellers for Children

At the time of publication, all websites referenced in this document were valid. However, due to the changing nature of the Internet, some addresses may change or the content become less relevant.

It's Your World Books

Africa: A Safari Through Its Amazing Nations!

Australia: The Land Down Under for Mates of All Ages!

Canada: The Maple Leaf Melting Pot Country!

China: A Great Wall Runs Thru It!

Egypt: An Ancient Land of Lore; a Modern Land of Oil and More!

France: The Ooh-La-La Country Everyone Loves!

Germany: The Country of Fairytale Castles and Cutting Edge Science!

Greece: A Volcanic Land of Ancient Olympic Origins!

India: Land of Six Senses and Intriguing Mystery!

Italy: The Country of Amazing Fountains and Awesome Arts!

Japan: An Island Country of Endless Intrigue!

Mexico: A Colorful Land of Exotic Culture!

Middle East: Ancient Countries of Current Events Headlines!

Russia: The Great Bear and Its Dramatic History!

South America: A Continent of Countries of Amazing Proportions!

United Kingdom: The Country of Ships, Sealing Wax, Cabbages, and Kings!

Other Carole Marsh Related Titles:

The Mystery at Mount Fuji

Japanese for Kids!

Table of Contents

A Letter from the Author

From the desk of
CAROLE MARSH

Hey kids,

It's your world! It really, really is! Of course, you already know that, don't you? You surf the 'net, listen to satellite radio, watch television shows and movies set all around the globe—kids today are much more "worldly" than in the past, and that's a good thing!

Now's a great time to learn something about another country—such as Japan. Why? Because one day, you might actually visit there (if you have not already!). You might go to school there—many colleges have ties with international schools around the globe. You might even go on to work in a foreign country!

Many companies have positions in other countries. Companies are "going global" as fast as they can. They have branch offices, manufacturing plants, and customer service centers scattered around the globe!

So, ready or not: YOU are a Citizen of the World! And you'll want to be a good one. How do you do that? You'll find out everything you can about that country, how it's the same, and how it's different from your own country. What language is spoken there? What customs do the people observe? What foods do they enjoy? What do they do for fun? What has happened in this part of the world, and what is happening there now? It's fun ... and the more you learn, the more you will enjoy whatever global opportunity comes your way!

This book is a good place to start your learning journey—so take advantage of the world—IT'S YOUR WORLD, after all ... and guess what? It's a BIG world, after all!

Happy traveling and learning,

Carole Marsh
Always with passport in hand!

Why Should We Care About Japan?

Japan is an amazing blend of beauty, culture, and strength! This island country lies in the North Pacific Ocean off the coast of Asia. It is extremely popular with tourists from around the globe. Everyone wants to see the gorgeous gardens, magnificent mountains, ancient temples, and plush palaces—and enjoy the graceful Japanese culture!

Japan is a vibrant nation, with a disciplined and highly educated workforce. It has one of the strongest economies in the world! And it is the home to Nintendo and Sony, makers of video games enjoyed all over the world!

One day, you might visit Japan to see the cherry blossoms in Kyoto, shop along Tokyo's bustling streets, or work for a Japanese company like Honda or Toyota. It could happen!

Write home about it!
What will your postcard from Japan say?

Top Fast Japan Facts!

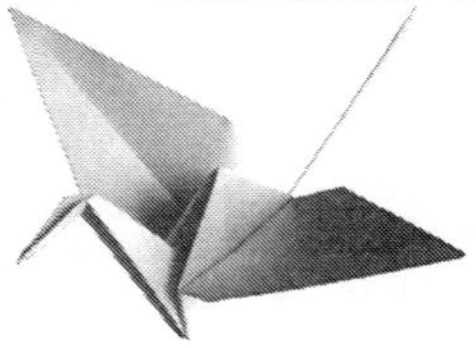

Important facts to remember about the country of Japan:

- Japan has a parliamentary government with a constitutional monarchy.
- Japan has an emperor and a prime minister.
- Japan calls itself "Nippon," which translates to "origin of the sun." Americans often refer to it as the "Land of the Rising Sun."
- Japan established its constitution in 1947.
- Japan is very strong in technology! It is the second most technologically powerful economy in the world after the United States.
- Japan has the third strongest economy in the world!
- Japan was an enemy of the United States in World War II. Today, Japan is a strong U.S. ally.
- Go fish! Japan's huge fishing fleet catches 15 percent of the fish caught around the world!
- Japan has a population of 127 million people.
- The capital of Japan is Tokyo.
- The official language of Japan is Japanese.
- The Japanese currency is the yen.
- Japan's national anthem is "Kimigayo."
- Japan has 188 volcanoes, and 40 of them are active! Earthquakes occur frequently in Japan.

Now, you figure out the rest!

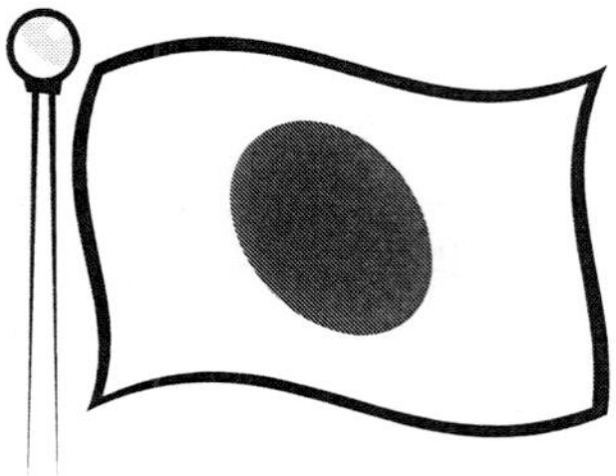

1. This is the Japanese ___ ___ ___ ___.

2. ___ ___ ___ ___ ___ ___ means "origin of the sun."

3. The ___ ___ ___ ___ ___ ___ ___ ___ ___ ___ of Japan is 127 million.

4. Mt. Fuji is one of Japan's many ___ ___ ___ ___ ___ ___ ___ ___ ___.

5. Japan has the ___ ___ ___ ___ ___ largest economy in the world.

6. The capital of Japan is ___ ___ ___ ___ ___.

Where in the World Is Japan?

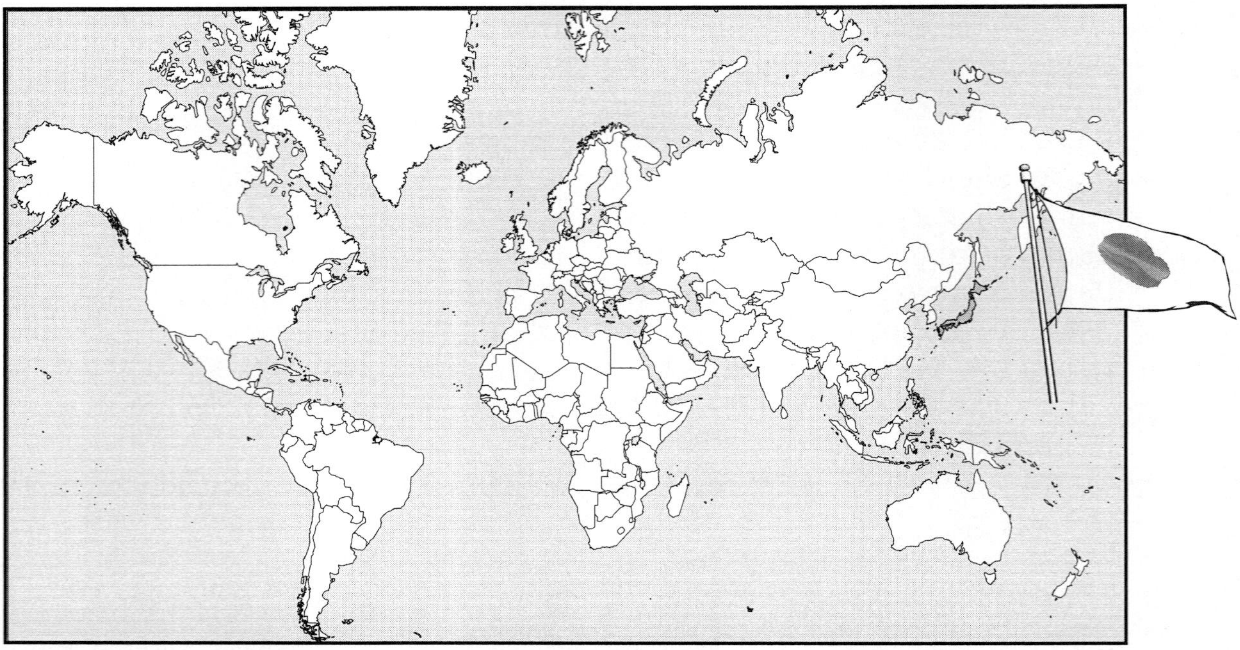

- Japan is an Asian country, east of China, North Korea, and South Korea.
- Japan is surrounded by the Pacific Ocean, the Sea of Japan, the Philippine Sea, and the East China Sea.
- Japan is made up of four main islands and 3,000 smaller islands. Honshu is the largest island.
- The Ryukyu Islands include the island of Okinawa. This island was the site of a famous World War II battle.
- Hokkaido, the northernmost island, is home to the Ainu people.
- Mountains cover about 75 percent of Japan's land.
- Four tectonic plates come together where Japan is located! That's why Japan experiences up to 1,500 earthquakes each year! The Kobe earthquake in 1995 killed more than 6,000 people!
- Japan has four distinct seasons.
- Japan is one of the world's most crowded countries! The majority of the people live in cities like Tokyo.

Do you know?

1. Because of its location, Japan has a very successful __________ industry.
   a. meat packing b. lumber c. fishing d. cotton

2. The highest point in Japan is:
   a. Mt. Everest b. Mt. McKinley c. Mt. Kobe d. Mt. Fuji

In the Beginning...

Japan has a truly fascinating history! The earliest known people, the Jomon Culture, were displaced by today's Japanese ancestors about 2,300 years ago. These new migrants organized themselves into small kingdoms. By about 500 C.E. they had become one kingdom and were ruled by an emperor. The emperor claimed that he was descended from the sun goddess.

Although the emperor was the absolute ruler, he held no real power. The power belonged to the aristocracy. Civil war broke out between ruling clans, and a military regime was installed. This regime was ruled by a *shogun* (the Japanese word for "general"), and a new class of warriors called *samurai* arose. The samurai protected and fought for the rulers of Japan. Sometimes they even gave their lives for them!

The last family of shoguns was called the Tokugawa clan. In the 1600s, these rulers expelled all foreigners, with the exception of a few Dutch and Chinese traders. Japan remained isolated from the rest of the world until the 1850s.

Crosswords!

Use your new knowledge to fill in the crossword puzzle.

Across

4 The __________ claimed to be descended from the sun goddess.

5 The last family of shoguns was the __________ clan.

Down

1 Japanese warriors were known as __________.

2 The earliest known people were from the __________ Culture.

3 The head of the military regime was called this.

Open Up and Let Us In!

Commodore Perry

Things changed for Japan in the 1800s! In 1853, American Commodore Matthew Perry arrived in Japan. He demanded that Japan open its doors to the West. The Japanese nation was no match for the heavily armed ships in the harbor, and the shogun agreed to Perry's terms. Some samurai were angry at the decision and rebelled. Their rebellion removed the shogun from power and Emperor Meiji took over.

The new Japanese government realized that the country needed to modernize! They built railroads, steamships, and factories. They changed both their education and government systems. Japan didn't necessarily become "Westernized." Instead, Japan took things from the West and made them Japanese!

Japan was an ally of the United States and Great Britain in World War I. But in World War II, Japan joined Germany and Italy as the Axis Powers. They fought against the United States and the Allies. On December 7, 1941, Japan attacked the U.S. Pacific Fleet at Pearl Harbor, Hawaii. Japan was defeated and finally surrendered in 1945.

After World War II, Japan rebuilt itself into an economic powerhouse! It provides the world with top-quality goods, including cameras, televisions, and automobiles!

Timeline
Number these events in the order they took place, first to last.

______ Admiral Perry arrives in Japan.

______ Japan allies with the United States and Great Britain.

______ New Japanese government modernizes Japan.

______ Japan becomes an economic powerhouse.

______ Samurai rebellion removes the shogun from power.

______ Japan joins Germany and Italy as an Axis Power.

______ Japan attacks the naval base at Pearl Harbor, Hawaii.

Famous Japanese Folks!

Matching!
Match these famous Japanese folks with their accomplishments.

_____ 1. I was the feudal military administrator from the 12th century to the 19th century. I was, as the emperor's military deputy, the actual ruler of Japan. My title originally meant "Commander of the Armies."

_____ 2. I am also known as Emperor Showa. I was the 124th emperor of Japan. After Japan surrendered at the end of WWII, I cooperated with the reorganization of the Japanese state. I lived to see Japan become a democracy and an industrial power.

_____ 3. On February 3, 1867, I succeeded my father, Emperor Komei, and this new era under my reign began. The name of my reign means "enlightened rule."

_____ 4. I am a Japanese warrior. I protected the Japanese nobility. My weapons included bows, arrows, spears, and swords.

_____ 5. Our names are Oda Nobunaga, Toyotomi Hideyoshi, and Tokugawa. We worked to unify the "warring states" of Japan. We lived at the end of the 15th century when Japan was in turmoil.

_____ 6. I was the Supreme Commander of the Allied war effort in the Pacific during World War II. I was also in charge of the Allied troops who stayed in Japan after WWII.

A. Three Great Unifiers

B. Emperor Meiji

C. Emperor Hirohito

D. General Douglas McArthur

E. Shogun

F. Samurai

Guts and Glory Japanese Style!

A. This is a traditional Japanese art where a single square of paper is folded to create shapes like animals or plants. The best-known origami shape, which many children learn from their parents or grandparents, is the crane. Other shapes include flowers, butterflies, crabs, and even difficult creations like Christmas trees.

B. This martial art was born in Japan. It is now known around the world as an Olympic sport where opponents often throw each other to the ground. It was started in 1882 by combining jujitsu, a form of wrestling, with mental discipline.

C. This art of arranging cut stems, leaves, and flowers in vases and other containers started in Japan more than seven centuries ago. People attend classes to learn how to place the flowers and stems in an exact way. It usually takes three to five years to learn these skills!

D. New Year in Japan would not be complete without this game, which is a bit like "pin-the-tail-on-the-donkey." Blindfolded players have an outline of a face with no features on the floor in front of them. The object of the game is to place paper cutouts in the shape of the eyes, nose, and mouth on the face!

E. In this ceremony, archers wear ancient hunting outfits. They shoot at wooden targets as they race by on horseback.

Mixed Up!
Match the paragraph to the word that the paragraph describes.

FUKU WARAI ____

____ **IKEBANA**

ORIGAMI ____

____ **YABUSAME**

____ **JUDO**

The Beautiful Bonsai!

Have you ever seen a Japanese *bonsai* tree? Once you do, you won't forget it! These amazing tiny trees are grown in containers and trimmed continually so they remain small. The word "bonsai" means "tray-planted tree."

Growing bonsai is a popular hobby in Japan. It is an example of the respect that the Japanese have for living things. It is also an expression of what they consider beautiful. It is much more involved than growing potted flowers and takes a lot longer—years, in fact!

The Japanese create bonsai trees from ones that grow in their country, like plum trees, cherry trees, pine trees, or maple trees. Growers do not let a bonsai tree grow more than three feet tall. The trees require continual trimming and shaping. Growers must also take them out of their pots, trim the roots, and put them in new pots from time to time.

Bonsai trees can live for more than 100 years! Families often pass them down through generations. What a beautiful gift to keep in the family!

Draw Me!
Get out your crayons. Draw a bonsai tree of your own design.

What a Pretty Pagoda!

The Japanese are very particular about their pagodas! A pagoda is a religious building in Japan and other countries where the Buddhist religion is popular. A pagoda looks like a tower with many stories. Often, each story looks like the one below it, but just a little smaller.

Pagodas are usually made of wood. They are very detailed and built to specific directions. They usually have an odd number of floors. Pagodas are so tall that they are often struck by lightning. For that reason, people considered them to be "spiritually charged!"

Later pagodas had a finial—or decorative rod—installed on the top. The finial attracts lightning to protect the pagoda from being hit and catching on fire. The finial is often made in the shape of a lotus flower, which has special meaning in Japan.

Write home about it!
Use the letters of Japanese Pagoda to create as many words with three letters or more as you can.

Japanese Pagoda

Tokyo Tower

Does this tower look familiar? You might think you're looking at the Eiffel tower in Paris, France. Actually, this tower is found in Tokyo, Japan! It's called Tokyo Tower, and it stands 1,091 feet tall—that's 28 feet taller than the Eiffel Tower!

Tokyo Tower broadcasts television and radio signals. But that's not all it does. Tourists and locals alike visit Tokyo Tower to be entertained! From two observation decks, you can see a panoramic view of all of Tokyo! Hungry? The tower boasts four restaurants, including a McDonald's! Kids love to visit the video arcade, aquarium, and wax museum featuring famous figures from the past! There's also a mini-amusement park with rides and games at the base of Tokyo Tower! What more could a kid ask for?

You can see Tokyo Tower from practically anywhere in Tokyo, especially at night.

The tower only weighs about 4,000 tons, which is extremely light compared to the Eiffel Tower which weighs 10,000 tons.

Under good weather conditions, Mount Fuji can be seen in the distance from the tower.

Every year at exactly 12 a.m. on New Year's, the sky around Tokyo Tower lights up with fireworks!

At the time Tokyo Tower was built, it was the tallest structure in Tokyo!

Create your very own travel pamphlet.
Concentrate on an area that interests you. Perhaps you enjoyed learning about the people. Or maybe it was the monuments that interested you. Fold a piece of paper into three sections. This will give you six areas on which to put information.

Bow Down!

Customs and culture vary widely from country to country. Sometimes they vary in different regions of the same country. Here are customs and cultural differences observed by the Japanese!

- Bowing is the common greeting. The more important a person is, the longer and deeper your bow should be!
- Slurping or making loud noises while you eat is considered a compliment!
- Visitors remove their shoes at the entrances to homes and businesses. Slippers are often provided to wear, instead!
- Public bathhouses are popular destinations. They are for soaking and relaxing only, so make sure you're clean before you get in!
- Steaming hot wet washcloths served before meals are used to wipe your hands, but never your face!
- The suffixes "san" or "sama" added to a last name are signs of respect.
- It is customary for women to give men chocolate on Valentine's Day. Men give women chocolate one month later on White Day!
- Roosters are considered sacred animals and are allowed to roam freely.

Create your own!
As we have seen, customs and cultural activities can help define who we are. Think about your family and friends and come up with some new customs for everyone to try.

Kanji? What's a Kanji?

The official language in Japan is Japanese. They use a combination of *Kanji* (simplified Chinese characters), *Hiragana*, and *Katakana* (for foreign words).

Match it up!

Below are some common Japanese phrases or words. See if you can match them to the English word.

futon

koen

funsui

sakura

sumo

tenisu

suki

sakka

gohan

cha iro

rice

skiing

brown

park

soccer

wrestler

portable bed

fountain

tennis

cherry blossom

実

神

活

愛

家

音

大

Happy Holidays!

Japan has 14 national holidays and multiple festivals. Every week, somewhere in Japan, there is a festival! What fun!

Coming-of-Age Day is the 2nd Monday in January and is for 20-year-olds. It marks the day that they become adults and can make decisions without their parents' consent. They march in a parade and are given gifts.

Shichi-go-san means seven-five-three in Japanese. This is a festival, celebrated on November 15th, where the people visit their favorite shrines and give thanks for their good fortune. Children who are ages seven, five, or three get special attention on these days.

There are many other shrine festivals throughout the year. Many of them are celebrated with floats, parades, dances, plays, bonfires, and fireworks shows.

Write it down!

Pretend you are visiting Japan. On the lines below, write a letter to your best friend. Tell him or her what a Japanese festival is like. How do you think their fireworks show would be the same as or different from an American one?

Japan on the Stage and in the Museums

The culture of art and theater in Japan dates back to more than 10,000 years. The "Land of the Rising Sun" is the birthplace of the world's most famous seascape, the *samurai* and *Naruto*.

2.

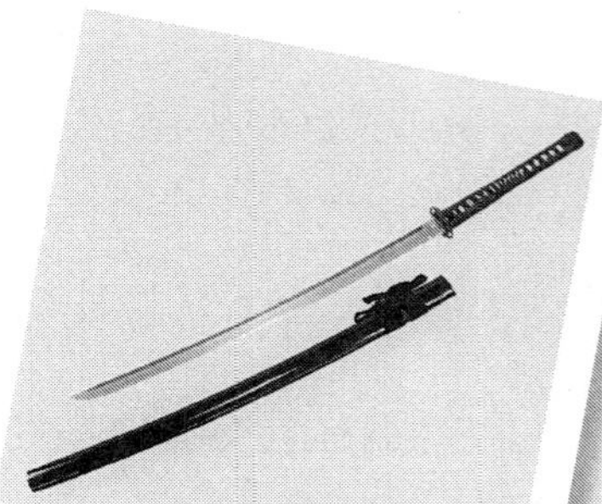

3.

Notes

1. *Anime* is Japanese cartoons. Characters evolve in a series and deal with complex issues.
2. Japan's most famous image is a seascape with Mt. Fuji called *The Great Wave* by Katsushika Hokusai.
3. One of the most delicate and complicated art forms in the world is the art of making Japanese samurai swords.
4. *Haiku* is a short poem that can be hard to understand because of its complex words and phrases.
5. *Kabuki* is a traditional Japanese form of theater. It was the popular culture of the townspeople, not of the higher social classes.

1.

5.

4.

What's for Dinner?

The Japanese enjoy one of the healthiest diets in the world. Fish, rice, and vegetables are the main ingredients of their meals. They use chopsticks to eat their meals. Here are a few things to eat if you visit Japan!

Sushi is a cold dish that consists of cooked rice and raw seafood. It is often wrapped in dried seaweed.

Miso soup is a soybean and grain broth served mostly at breakfast.

Sukiyaki is a dish of thin slices of meat, served with noodles, vegetables, and tofu.

Green tea is a favorite drink enjoyed with meals.

RECIPE

Always ask an adult for help when cooking!

Peanut Cookies

INGREDIENTS

- ½ cup margarine
- 2 eggs
- 1¼ cups cake flour
- margarine to grease pan
- 1 cup brown sugar
- ½ teaspoon vanilla extract
- ½ cup or more peanuts
- ½ cup flour

DIRECTIONS

1. In a mixing bowl, combine margarine and brown sugar with a mixer until fluffy.
2. Beat in the eggs and vanilla.
3. Mix in the flour.
4. Add peanuts and stir lightly with a spoon.
5. With a teaspoon of dough, form dough into small balls.
6. Place doughballs onto a greased baking sheet.
7. Flatten balls in a crisscross pattern with a fork dipped in flour.
8. Refrigerate baking sheet and dough cookies for about 20 minutes.
9. Bake cookies at 320° F for 15 to 20 minutes until lightly browned.

Makes 2 dozen cookies

Survival of the Strongest!

They're big...they're strong...they're sumo wrestlers! Sumo wrestling is a sport where a man attempts to force another man out of a circular ring or to touch the ground with anything other than the bottom of his feet. It is a professional sport only in Japan. The Japanese consider sumo a modern martial art—a type of combat.

Sumo wrestling started as a type of religious dance, where a human was said to be actually wrestling with a divine Shinto spirit, or *kami*. The original wrestlers—called *rikishi*—were samurai who competed with each other in order to win money.

Today, professional sumo wrestling bouts are put on by the Japan Sumo Association. Only former rikishi are allowed to train new rikishi. The rikishi have special wrestling names. (What would your wrestling name be?) Professional sumo consists of approximately 550 rikishi divided into six divisions. The top division, called *Makuuchi*, includes the top 42 wrestlers in the sport. There are 15 bouts in each competition.

Sumo rikishi have a lot of rules they must follow or they will be kicked out of the sport. They are not even allowed to drive a car! They are told what to eat, when to eat, and must be in bed at a certain time every night. Trainees have to get up at 5 o'clock in the morning! It doesn't sound like much fun, but rikishi are famous and popular people in Japan.

Figure it out!

Figure out the answers to these questions about sumo wrestling.

1. There are 550 rikishi in six divisions, and 42 of those rikishi are Makuuchi, the top-ranked sumo wrestlers who can never be dropped to a lower rank. How many rikishi can be dropped to a lower rank?

   ____

2. There are 15 bouts in each sumo match. How many bouts must the winner win?

   ____

Fast Fact:
Konishiki Yasokichi is a Hawaiian born Japanese-Samoan sumo wrestler and is nicknamed "The Dump Truck." He was the first foreign-born wrestler to reach *ozeki*, the second highest rank in the sport.

A Cup of Tea in the Garden, Please!

A beautiful garden is a relaxing place to be! To the Japanese, gardening is an art and a way to express feelings. Gardens show up in Japanese history books as far back as the 6th century. Early gardens contained artificial hills, ornamental pools, rocks, and many other features like Japanese gardens do today. Later, the Chinese taught the Japanese how to build fancier gardens with animals, birds, and fish. These gardens were used as places for feasts and parties given by noblemen.

From 1185 to 1392, Zen Buddhists built gardens as a place for them to meditate. The Zen gardens were much simpler than the noblemen's gardens. They included stones, water, and evergreens. After 1392, and until the late 16th century, even simpler gardens became popular. They were made entirely of flat stones! They were called rock gardens. After the 16th century, fancy gardens were grown again. Today, you can still see examples of all these types of gardens in Japan.

Ryoanji Zen Temple in Kyoto

The Japanese tea ceremony combines the love of gardens with tea, a popular drink. This ceremony, or *Cha-no-yu,* which means "hot water for tea," is a favorite tradition in Japan. In 1191, a Japanese Buddhist monk—a holy man—planted a tea garden. He also wrote the first book about the Japanese tea ceremony.

The tea ceremony is supposed to help bring harmony, respect, purity, and tranquility to the people who take part in it. The flowers, trees, birds, butterflies, and the sound of trickling water from a garden fountain add to the calm, serene experience.

Word Fun!

Plant the word in the correct garden! Some words will go in both!

birds, fountains, rocks, evergreens, butterflies, water, cherry trees, roses

Zen Garden	Tea Garden
______________	______________
______________	______________
______________	______________
______________	______________
______________	______________

Japan Did It First!

Just Noodling Around!
In 1958, Momofuku Ando marketed the first package of pre-cooked instant noodles, called ramen.

Sing Us a Song!
Daisuke Inoue invented the karaoke machine in 1971. Karaoke means "empty orchestra."

Look to the Stars!
Kunitomo Ikkansai, built Japan's first reflective telescope in 1831.

Solving Problems Before They Start!
Sakichi Toyoda invented a "smart" loom that could automatically catch mistakes and stop the machine.

Word Fun!

This is fun to do with someone else. Ask a friend for words to substitute for the blanks in the story. Their word substitutions will have a humorous effect when the resulting story is then read aloud.

I want to be the first person to ______________________ (ACTION VERB)

across ______________________ (COUNTRY)! I've been training for this

since ______________ (MONTH). I'm in ______________ (ADJECTIVE) shape.

My ______________________ (ADJECTIVE) adventure will begin on

______________________ (FAVORITE HOLIDAY). I won't be hard to miss;

I'll be the one wearing a ______________________ (COLOR)

______________________ (ARTICLE OF CLOTHING) and a pair of matching

______________________ (FOOTWEAR). My faithful friends

______________________ (FAMOUS ATHLETE) and

______________________ (CARTOON CHARACTER) will be there to cheer for me.

I'm bringing my ______________________ (NOUN) along for good luck.

I'm confident I'll be the first!

He Is a Real Transformer!
Professor Shigeo Hirose designed many types of robots. His most impressive robot, called the "ninja," can climb buildings and mountain slopes.

That's My Type!
Many Japanese wanted to use the typewriter, but it didn't support Japanese text. In 1929, Kyota Sugimoto patented the first Japanese version that used 2,400 characters.

A Magnificent Mountain!

Mount Fuji is Japan's highest mountain. It is also a sacred symbol of Japan—and a volcano!

Mount Fuji is 3,776 meters or 12,388 feet high. It is one of Japan's "Three Holy Mountains," along with Mount Tate and Mount Haku. Mount Fuji is still an active volcano, although the last time it erupted was on December 16, 1707. Lava and ash flowed from the mountain for more than two weeks!

Mount Fuji's name means "everlasting life." Shrines and temples surround the mountain, and its entire base is a national park dotted with five lakes. Japanese people climb the mountain in July and August as a religious practice. It's cold up there, though—the temperatures in summer only reach 5 or 6 degrees Celsius (41 to 43 degrees Fahrenheit). People often climb the mountain at night so they can watch the sunrise in the morning!

Word Fun!

Write 5 questions you could ask someone who lives near Mt. Fuji. We've given you an example to get you started.

Example: Do you go swimming in the lakes around Mt. Fuji?

1. ______________________________?
2. ______________________________?
3. ______________________________?
4. ______________________________?
5. ______________________________?

Japan Is "Technology Central"

Do you like to play video games? Do you like to watch television? Do you like to take pictures with a camera that automatically focuses for you? If you answered "yes," you can thank the country of Japan!

After World War II, Japan had to rebuild its country and its economy. The Japanese recovery is often called an "economic miracle!" One of the greatest areas of Japanese success is technology. Japanese innovation and quality products have had a major impact on people around the world. Have you heard of Honda or Toyota cars? How about Nintendo video games? How about Panasonic or Mitsubishi televisions? Japanese products are everywhere!

One reason that the Japanese are so innovative is because they have to be! Japan is a small, mountainous country with few natural resources like oil to make gasoline. Since Japan has to import its gasoline, it is very expensive. So, the Japanese have developed fuel-efficient cars! The Japanese have also created lightweight materials to build tall buildings. They need them to house their many people on a small amount of land!

Another reason for Japan's success is its people! The Japanese culture puts a great emphasis on discipline, hard work, and education. The Japanese work hard, and their country has been successful because of it!

Revealing Answer!

Follow the instructions to reveal a technology called *keitai denwa* that is very popular in Japan!

1. Cross off the first and last letters.
2. Cross off the letter that represents the Roman numeral 5.
3. Cross off the fifth, 11th, and 13th letters.
4. Cross off the second B and both Rs.
5. Cross off the letter Y.
6. Cross off the fourth letter from the right.

AMVODBBIYLFEGPRRHVOYNZESB

____

Sleeping in a Capsule!

Capsule Hotel

Have you ever spent the night in a hotel room? If so, you probably tossed your suitcase in a corner, took a shower in a roomy bathroom, and slept on a nice big bed! Well, in Japan, you wouldn't enjoy any of those things if you stayed in a capsule hotel!

In a Japanese capsule hotel, guests sleep in a small sleeping chamber just big enough for a twin-size bed! These chambers are called capsules. They're just about the size of a refrigerator box! Each capsule has a television, a radio, an alarm clock, and a light. Guests pull down a screen at the end of the capsule to close themselves in for the night. Luggage is stowed in lockers, and guests share shower rooms and bathrooms.

Most visitors to capsule hotels are Japanese businessmen who work late and do not have time to go home for the night. Foreign travelers also like them because they are very inexpensive. But if you go to a capsule hotel, make sure you don't mind being confined to very small spaces!

Fast Fact:
Capsules feature lots of buttons and knobs to control the television, lights, and alarm. Guests can reach them all while lying down!

Cross it off!
Starting with the first letter, cross off every other letter to reveal the name of something you might need in a capsule hotel. After all, there aren't any doors!

Z E R A M R X P S L N U T G Q S

____

Terrific Train Travel!

Imagine hopping on a train and traveling to any city or town! You can do that in Japan! The major cities on Honshu, the main island of Japan, are all connected by a system of eight different *shinkansen* (bullet train) lines.

***Oshiya* helping commuters board a rush-hour train in Tokyo**

These amazing trains travel incredibly fast—up to 185 mph! Businesspeople and students use them to travel from their homes outside of the cities to their jobs or schools in the cities.

There's a system of train and subway lines within cities, too! The *zaraisen*, or regular train and subway lines, run at much slower speeds (80 mph max.). Many people living in Japanese cities don't even own a car! With 17,000 miles of rail crisscrossing the country (that's further than halfway around the world!), who needs a car?

Commuters, shoppers, sightseers, and students use this very safe and punctual form of transportation. In fact, it's not uncommon at all to see kindergarteners taking the trains to school by themselves!

Japanese trains are almost always on time. A delay of even five minutes is followed by a sincere apology over the loudspeaker! Even during the morning and evening rush hours, the trains run on time. But be ready to be packed in like sardines by the *oshiya*, or official pushers!

Fast Fact:
Decorating the outside of certain bullet trains is becoming a Japanese trend. The Pokemon character, Pikachu, is featured on the outside of one bullet train.

Figure it out!
Read the phrases below. Write "S" if the statement describes shinkansen trains. Write "Z" if it describes zaraisen trains.

____ 1. Bullet train
____ 2. Kindergarteners ride
____ 3. 80 miles per hour
____ 4. 185 miles per hour
____ 5. Train line from homes into cities
____ 6. Train line within cities

Japanese Fashion–the Comfy Kimono!

It's a dress. It's a robe. No, it's a *kimono,* the national clothing of Japan! Kimono, in Japanese, means "thing to wear," so originally, kimono meant any type of clothing. Later, the word came to describe a certain type of clothing that was like a robe, wrapped around the body, and belted at the waist with a sash called an obi.

Kimonos have collars and long, wide sleeves. They are usually made of brightly colored fabric with elegant pictures and patterns. Never wear sneakers with your kimono! Kimonos are worn with split-toe socks, called *tabi,* and Japanese sandals, called *zori.*

Both men and women can wear a kimono. Today, women wear them most often when attending a wedding, tea ceremony, or other formal event. Sumo wrestlers are required to wear them when they appear in public. (Apparently kimonos come in extra-extra-large sizes!)

Dress Up!

Help Christina get dressed for her tour of Japan. Here are some clothing styles you might see in Japan today. Choose which outfit she'll wear. Color the clothing, and draw a line from the piece of clothing to Christina, or cut out the clothing and dress her up!

Assorted Architecture!

Figure it out!

Use the following clues to figure out the name of this famous building in Himeji, Hyogo Prefecture, Japan.

- It took eight years to build this fortress, from 1601 to 1609.
- It has survived wars and earthquakes and is a popular tourist attraction.
- It is also called the "White Egret Castle" because its white walls look like a flock of flying egrets.
- It is surrounded by a maze to confuse enemies who tried to attack it!
- It was built from parts of other buildings because construction materials were not easy to get at that time. The builders even used old gravestones in the construction!
- It was built of wood, but the builders covered the wood with white plaster to make it harder to burn down. Its foundation is made of large loose stones, which has helped it survive earthquakes.

As They Say in Japanese...

Here are a few Japanese words you may already know. Why? Because we use them as "English" words all the time!

karaoke: entertainment where an amateur singer sings along to recorded music

ninja: a spy or assassin in old Japan. Ninjas are famous for wearing black clothing and scarves to hide their appearance at night

origami: brightly colored paper folded into a variety of shapes

samurai: a warrior of old Japan

sudoku: a number placement puzzle

sushi: in Japan, sushi is vinegared rice usually topped with other ingredients, including fish, various meats, and vegetables

tempura: seafood and vegetables coated in an egg/flour batter and deep-fried

teriyaki: meat broiled with soy sauce. In America, it has come to mean the name of the sauce on the meat

Toyota: a brand of Japanese car

tsunami: a tidal wave, usually the result of an undersea earthquake

Wii: pronounced as the English pronoun "we," is a home video game console

yen: Japanese money

Further Resources

U.S. Embassy in Japan
1-10-5 Akasaka
Minato-ku, Tokyo 107-8420
Phone: (03) 3224-5000 / DSN 224-5000 Switchboard
Fax: (03) (03)3224-5914 / DSN 224-5914

United Nations
2 United Nations Plaza
New York, NY 10017

Japan National Tourist Organization
10th Floor, Tokyo Kotsu Kaikan Building, 2-10-1 Yurakucho
Chiyoda-ku, Tokyo 100-0006
Phone: +81-3-3201-3331

Tokyo Convention and Visitor's Bureau
tcvbinfo@tcvb.or.jp

Interesting Websites

http://english.taipei.gov.tw/zoo

http://mountfujiguide.com/

http://www.nagasaki.world-guides.com/

http://www.japaneselifestyle.com/

Answer Key

Page 7
1. flag, 2. Nippon, 3. population, 4. volcanoes, 5. third, 6. Tokyo

Page 8
1. c, 2. d

Page 9

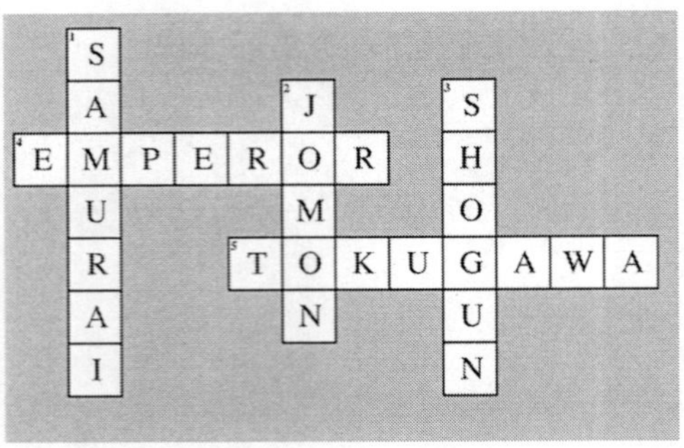

Page 10
1, 4, 3, 6, 2, 5, 7

Page 11
1. E, 2. C, 3. B, 4. F, 5. A, 6. D

Page 12
fuku warai-D, Ikebana-C, origami-A, Yabusame-E, Judo-B

Page 17

futon	portable bed
koen	park
funsui	fountain
sakura	cherry blossom
sumo	wrestler
tenisu	tennis
suki	skiing
sakka	soccer
gohan	rice
cha iro	brown

Page 21
1. 508, 2. 8

Page 22

Zen Garden	**Tea Garden**
Rocks	Birds
Evergreens	Fountains
Water	Butterflies
	Cherry Trees
	Roses
	Rocks

Page 25
Mobile Phones

Page 26
earplugs

Page 27
1. S
2. Z
3. Z
4. S
5. S
6. Z